Getting Started with Flurry Analytics

Utilize Flurry Analytics to optimize and monetize your applications more effectively

Bhanu Birani

BIRMINGHAM - MUMBAI

Getting Started with Flurry Analytics

First published: December 2013

Production Reference: 1161213

Published by Packt Publishing Ltd.

Livery Place
35 Livery Street
Birmingham B3 2PB, UK.

ISBN 978-1-78217-712-8

www.packtpub.com

Cover Image by Sheetal Aute (sheetala@packtpub.com)

Credits

Author
Bhanu Birani

Reviewers
Emil Atanasov

Benjamin Bahrenburg

Tom Meinlschmidt

Acquisition Editor
Saleem Ahmed

Luke Presland

Commissioning Editors
Nikhil Chinnari

Poonam Jain

Technical Editor
Nadeem N. Bagban

Copy Editors
Alisha Aranha

Brandt D'Mello

Deepa Nambiar

Project Coordinator
Suraj Bist

Proofreader
Ameesha Green

Indexer
Rekha Nair

Production Coordinator
Adonia Jones

Cover Work
Adonia Jones

About the Author

Bhanu Birani has four years of experience in the software industry and a lifetime association with the technical industry. After years of programming in different programming languages, he started developing applications for iOS devices. He started software development during his college years and was really interested in learning new technologies in the market. He then joined a software company and started developing games for them, focusing on artificial intelligence development in games.

I would like to dedicate this book to my family, who gave me the courage and confidence to write this book and supported me throughout the entire process. I would also like to send a special thanks to my mom (Neelu Birani) and dad (Prakash Birani) for their relentless efforts to assist me in every way imaginable, as well as for helping me keep my life together. Finally, I would like to thank my friend Luke P. Issac for helping me on this project and encouraging me when it seemed too difficult to complete.

About the Reviewers

Benjamin Bahrenburg is an author, blogger, and technology director. Ben specializes in building enterprise solutions using mobile technologies, geo location services, and domain-specific languages. Over the last decade, he has provided enterprise mobility solutions for numerous Fortune 100 organizations. Ben is a published writer who has authored several articles and *Appcelerator Titanium Business Application Development Cookbook*, Packt Publishing, which provides best practices and recipes for successful enterprise cross-platform mobile development.

Ben spends much of his time blogging and speaking about mobile, enterprise, and open source development at http://bencoding.com. You can also reach him on Twitter at http://twitter.com/bencoding.

Tom Meinlschmidt started his professional career in 1998. He is a senior software developer with expertise in Ruby and Ruby on Rails. He has developed various types of applications for a variety of companies, and he specializes in web and iOS applications. He is also interested in new technologies and modern programming languages, 3D modeling, rendering, and embedded systems (ARM). When he's not working on his Mac, he's flying as a commercial helicopter pilot. You can find his blog at tom.meinlschmidt.org.

www.PacktPub.com

Support files, eBooks, discount offers and more

You might want to visit www.PacktPub.com for support files and downloads related to your book.

Did you know that Packt offers eBook versions of every book published, with PDF and ePub files available? You can upgrade to the eBook version at www.PacktPub.com and as a print book customer, you are entitled to a discount on the eBook copy. Get in touch with us at service@packtpub.com for more details.

At www.PacktPub.com, you can also read a collection of free technical articles, sign up for a range of free newsletters and receive exclusive discounts and offers on Packt books and eBooks.

http://PacktLib.PacktPub.com

Do you need instant solutions to your IT questions? PacktLib is Packt's online digital book library. Here, you can access, read and search across Packt's entire library of books.

Why Subscribe?

- Fully searchable across every book published by Packt
- Copy and paste, print and bookmark content
- On demand and accessible via web browser

Free Access for Packt account holders

If you have an account with Packt at www.PacktPub.com, you can use this to access PacktLib today and view nine entirely free books. Simply use your login credentials for immediate access.

Instant Updates on New Packt Books

Get notified! Find out when new books are published by following @PacktEnterprise on Twitter, or the *Packt Enterprise* Facebook page.

Table of Contents

Preface

Flurry Analytics provides you with an independent way of tracking your application, with a seamlessly user-friendly, web-based interface to access all the statistical data. Flurry emphasizes providing better control for management over their application and in turn, helps with management decisions by improving product roadmaps to have better user acquisition, engagement, and retention.

This book will teach you the fundamentals of getting started with Flurry Analytics and integrating it in your iOS application. As this book is meant to quickly get you familiar with Flurry and will cover all the important aspects of Flurry Analytics and its iOS SDK, it will cover a lot of subjects very quickly. Throughout the book, we will be dealing with the direct implementations by using effective examples and code. This approach will help you implement the example code and integrate the same thing in to your project quickly.

Working with Flurry is easy. This book will allow you to set up your application in no time. The book explains all the topics using code and includes lots of useful tips that explain all the little parts of Flurry.

One of the key points is segmentation and funnel, which helps you track your application usage for specific user paths. Flurry works for multiplatform applications and web development as well. Flurry also helps you to increase application monetization with better user retention and engagement strategies.

What this book covers

This book is written to get you familiar with the basic fundamentals of using Flurry to fulfil your application analytics. To achieve this, the book is organized in easy to understand examples and codes.

Chapter 1, Getting Ready with Flurry, starts by looking at advantages of using Flurry Analytics. Then, you will learn about configuring your account and applications on Flurry and Flurry's integration in your project. Finally, we will end the chapter by adding some code so you can start tracking applications on Flurry.

Chapter 2, Tracking Applications, explains the ways to set up goals to track your application on Flurry. We'll learn about various ways to track application data in terms of time spent by users on the application, module-based tracking, and tracking the specific version of application.

Chapter 3, Data Analysis, will explain the ways to analyze the data generated by Flurry. This chapter also explains the various features of Flurry that help when analyzing data to generate significant information.

Chapter 4, Technical Analytics, starts by exploring the ways to track application crashes and reading crash analytics data. This chapter also explains how to gather data to stabilize your application. Then finally, we will learn about data usage and its advantages in market analysis.

Chapter 5, Using Your Data, starts by explaining the ways in which the data generated by Flurry can be used to strengthen strategies. Then we will learn about various ways to use the features provided by Flurry to enhance its analytic capabilities. Then we will learn about Push sending options. Finally, we will learn some ways to read the statistics and graphs generated by Flurry.

What you need for this book

You'll need the following things to start writing applications for iOS devices using Parse SDK:

- An Intel-based Mac running Leopard (OS X 10.5.3 or higher)
- Xcode IDE
- You must be enrolled as an iPhone developer in order to test the example projects in your device

Who this book is for

If you want to instantly add analytics to your application, then this book is for you. In this book, you will learn to use Flurry Analytics to track your application and read the data generated to produce significant results. This book helps you to look beyond the number of downloads of your application to actually investigate the way users are interacting with your application.

This book uses Objective-C as its main language, so a basic knowledge of Objective-C is a must. This book assumes that you understand the fundamentals of object-oriented programming and programming in general.

This book is designed to get you started using Flurry Analytics with an iPhone or iPad, so you should be familiar with the iPhone or iPad itself. The iPhone is a great platform for programming as it looks nice and feels nice. Flurry helps you to add analytics to your application in order to track user behavior and improve user retention and engagement.

Conventions

In this book, you will find a number of styles of text that distinguish between different kinds of information. Here are some examples of these styles, and an explanation of their meaning.

Code words in text are shown as follows: "In `AppDelegate.h` file, find the `application:didFinishLaunchingWithOptions:` method and find where we are registering for push notifications".

A block of code is set as follows:

```
- (BOOL)application:(UIApplication *)application
 didFinishLaunchingWithOptions:(NSDictionary *)launchOptions {
    ...
    // Register for push notifications
    [application registerForRemoteNotificationTypes:
                                UIRemoteNotificationTypeBadge |
                                UIRemoteNotificationTypeAlert |
                                UIRemoteNotificationTypeSound];
    ...
}
```

All the command-line input or output is written as follows:

```
curl -s https://www.parse.com/downloads/cloud_code/installer.sh |
  sudo /bin/bash
```

New terms and important words are shown in bold. Words that you see on the screen, for example, in menus or dialog boxes appear in the text like this: "After clicking on the **Event Summary,** you can see the list of events you have created".

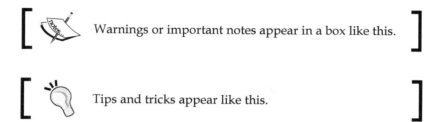

Warnings or important notes appear in a box like this.

Tips and tricks appear like this.

Reader feedback

Feedback from our readers is always welcome. Let us know what you think about this book—what you liked or may have disliked. Reader feedback is important for us to develop titles that you really get the most out of.

To send us general feedback, simply send an e-mail to feedback@packtpub.com, and mention the book title via the subject of your message.

If there is a topic that you need and would like to see us publish, please send us a note in the **SUGGEST A TITLE** form on www.packtpub.com or e-mail suggest@packpub.com.

If there is a topic that you have expertise in and you are interested in either writing or contributing to a book, see our author guide on www.packtpub.com/authors.

Customer support

Now that you are the proud owner of a Packt book, we have a number of things to help you to get the most from your purchase.

Downloading the example code

You can download the example code files for all Packt books you have purchased from your account at http://www.packtpub.com. If you purchased this book elsewhere, you can visit http://www.packtpub.com/support and register to have the files e-mailed directly to you.

Errata

Although we have taken every care to ensure the accuracy of our content, mistakes do happen. If you find a mistake in one of our books—maybe a mistake in the text or the code—we would be grateful if you would report this to us. By doing so, you can save other readers from frustration and help us improve subsequent versions of this book. If you find any errata, please report them by visiting http://www.packtpub.com/submit-errata, selecting your book, clicking on the **errata submission form** link, and entering the details of your errata. Once your errata are verified, your submission will be accepted and the errata will be uploaded on our website, or added to any list of existing errata, under the Errata section of that title. Any existing errata can be viewed by selecting your title from http://www.packtpub.com/support.

Piracy

Piracy of copyright material on the Internet is an ongoing problem across all media. At Packt, we take the protection of our copyright and licenses very seriously. If you come across any illegal copies of our works, in any form, on the Internet, please provide us with the location address or website name immediately so that we can pursue a remedy.

Please contact us at copyright@packtpub.com with a link to the suspected pirated material.

We appreciate your help in protecting our authors, and our ability to bring you valuable content.

Questions

You can contact us at questions@packtpub.com if you are having a problem with any aspect of the book, and we will do our best to address it.

1
Getting Ready with Flurry

Before getting into the details of Flurry and its analytics services, we will learn the reason behind using analytics in mobile applications. Then, we will learn about its setup and integration in our project. By the end of this chapter, you will know how to set up your project on Flurry along with its integration in your project.

In this chapter, we will learn the following:

- What, why, and how to use analytics
- The advantages of using analytics
- Setting up your account and application in Flurry

About Analytics

While developing mobile applications, most people start with strong strategies, great design, and solid development for their application. Above all of these, analytics serves as a measure to gauge the value of all the efforts you have put into the application's development. We all know that this is the generation of smartphones; they are going to penetrate all aspects of our lives and will have a significant impact on our day-to-day lives. This provides developers, management, and other partners an opportunity to measure user impact and behavior using application analytics. As compared to all other industries, the mobile application industry is young. Flurry provides good analytics data to help you understand the industry better.

Using analytics will help you in the following ways:

- Start using application analytics long before pushing the application to store
- Make a difference in how you and your users are using the application
- Use market analysis to avoid the mistakes already committed by your competitors
- Analytics data lasts longer than your mobile app; it helps you to understand the market structure and plan strategies accordingly

The importance of Analytics in the use of applications

Analytics allows you to analyze the impact of your application on your customers. It helps management in taking vital decisions on project scalability to meet the current market demands. It also helps project managers and management members avoid unforeseen problems.

- **How Analytics are used**: Earlier, companies used historical data and evidence to forecast application trends. Nowadays, there is a revolutionary change in data information as we have the Internet and social media in place, which provide large-scale data and make it difficult to extract useful information. Analytics provides an effective means of crunching useful data from large amounts of data.

- **How Analytics improve applications**: Higher level management can track the direct progress of a project by accessing charts, which easily display data and comparisons. Analytics provide directions to management by telling them whether the milestones are met and the project costing is in control. It also provides detailed analysis for a broader view. Let's say you want to know about the total time spent by a user on your application and what small shift can improve the outcome. Analytics helps management in prioritizing such tasks to maximize productivity.

- **How organizations can best use Analytics**: Analytics help managers assess the viability of their applications and gauge the applications that meet the benchmarks. It's important for managers to gather all these records and data for projects important to check how these changes in the application impact customers.

- **Using Analytics for projecting outcomes**: Analytical data provides better insights to an organization about delays in product delivery to customers, and how it affects the company profit.

- **Using Analytics to create strategies**: Data helps in forecasting and planning resources and requirements. It also empowers organizations to see the potential in the application idea and its scope in the market. It provides a better way to create business strategies rather than assuming and forecasting to lay strategies.

Flurry is a strong and powerful analytics agent that provides a **Software Development Kit (SDK)** for all the major platforms such as iOS and Android. It allows developers to track their application usage and track users' activities to improve the overall user experience. Flurry easy to integrate with your project.

Note that the iOS SDK will only work with Xcode 4.5 or higher. If you need the SDK for an older version of Xcode, you can e-mail Flurry support at support@flurry.com.

The **CoreLocation** framework is not required for the Flurry iOS SDK as it doesn't detect the GPS location by default. However, if developers want to track a user's location data, they can use **CCLocationManager** to set the GPS location data information on Flurry Analytics.

If geo-tracking is only for the purpose of analytics, it is not well accepted by Apple and the app can be rejected. So be careful. If you want to geo-track the user, you should have a geo-based feature in your app; otherwise, your app may have some problems during the Appstore approval phase.

Flurry Analytics must be called in a main thread as it's supported only on the main thread.

The advantages of using Analytics

You can get detailed knowledge of customers' behavior very quickly and with little effort using Flurry's Analytics service. Here are a few advantages of using Analytics:

- Keeps track of your app customers and provides their satisfaction with mobile analytics.

- Provides metrics to crunch data for a business development model.

- Flurry has been a mobile analytics company for over four years. It offers free services with no data limitations and it owns the mobile data it processes.

- Keeps your fingers on the pulse of your business with Flurry mobile Analytics.

- Helps you to know your customers better.

- Helps you in customer acquisition management, ad attribution management, and targeting in nature and retargeting campaigns.

Organizations usually apply analytics to business data to develop better insight into business goals and targets. Specifically, areas covered in analytics include enterprise decision and strategy management, retail management and store analytics, web analytics, application promotion marketing, and sales analytics. All the analytics require extensive computation, powerful algorithms, and software used for analytics, which are the most common methods in today's computer science, statistics, and mathematics.

Tracking social productivity

Flurry provides you with social analytics that is very useful in current market. High engagement in social media has raised the requirements for social media marketing in organizations. Social media marketing has now become the key component for marketing. Analytics helps to determine the best social place to publicize the application and the location from where the application targets a large number of customers.

There is a list of social media giants in the market on which you should start a campaign to achieve significant results. A few of the supported platforms are Facebook, Instagram, Twitter, LinkedIn, Google +, Pinterest, and so on.

Flurry also provides you with monetary value conversions, which helps you to know which social site is more productive and which is less productive. These results will help you to customize your strategies accordingly and further strengthen your marketing in the required social media. Along with these updates, you can also focus on your weaknesses to overcome them and prove your business logic to strengthen the weak parts.

Determining unique visitors

It's sometimes important to know how many new visitors your application has to track its growth rate. It's even more helpful when we know the growth rate of the application for the time period chosen by us. Let's say that the result is 100; this means that 100 unique users visit your application everyday. This number is directly associated with your rank in search engines.

Determining user behavior

Determining user behavior is one of the most important analytics as users are the ones for whom the application is developed. Flurry Analytics provides you with a better way to understand users' behavior while they using the application, which helps you to identify which sections or screens of your application are frequently accessed by the users. This reflects user engagement level and the flow they are traversing. You will also get data that tells you the type of device that your users are using the application on, along with the time they spend using your application. This information is useful to improve marketing plans.

Monitoring the performance of your ads

We are now in the era of online media advertising, which can add success to your journey. The difficult part of the application process is reaching its customers. Many applications use ads as their main monetary source. Marketing helps you to reach and scale your user base. You will definitely capture a larger market than applications that are not marketed at all.

Ads performance is also dependent on an effective marketing campaign. Flurry provides you various advertising channels to track your ads performance. Advertising analytics help you to track all your possible advertising channels such as social ads, e-mails, and banner ads.

This feature of Flurry also helps you to track the **AdWords** campaign,by which a user can get a track of all the ads and the number of clicks on the ads, how many times the ads is been clicked by user and know which words or terms have better impact on users and which one is non-productive. In the AdWords marketing strategy, you can provide auto tagging to your advertising campaign, which helps you to analyze the impact of words and placement of ads on your landing page.

Flurry report data provides you with a better way of relaunching your marketing campaign with rich insight into your customers. You can pinpoint prospects with the major features and points of your products, thus allowing an effective target for your ads with proper synchronization of interests.

Determining your content sources

Flurry provides you with effective content sources to analyze the screen or section of the application that gets high-user traffic. This information can be used to determine which content is most valuable to users and to develop similar content to make the application preferable to the visitors' needs.

Evaluating traffic flow to your application

Flurry is useful in finding out information about the various sources of incoming traffic to your application to help determine your marketing strategy. You can also find popular links and keywords that are used by visitors while searching for specific products in search engines. This can be useful for maximizing the results of your e-mail marketing campaign for the success of your promotional efforts. Besides, this method of tracking users' activities on the application can be immensely useful to help you cater to the specific needs and requirements of your customers.

Using Analytics will help users to trace their activities and follow up, with their interests and visited channels on the application.

- **Tracking activity**: Where do your visitors come from? This covers all the user activity, which includes the place from where your visitors are coming frequently along with their ways they are interacting with your application. It can be from social media, such as Twitter and LinkedIn, or through websites or blogs.

- **Track response**: Are you pushing a message based on user interest and the number of visits you are getting from your message? Are your messages interesting enough and getting user attention? After launching a message on your application, how long is it staying on the application? Is your message informative enough? Count the number of times a user comes back to your application. Count the number of the people who get into your sales funnel. Are such people buying your services and have you got the sales? This includes the tracking of the user's response on your ads, and your application. This also includes the response from the user about your messages that you are pushing in your application. This section tracks the way user interacts with your messages.

- **Gather your users' demographics**: You can get the age, gender, and location of your users.

- **Tracking user location when they interacted with the application**: It should be as precise as possible, such as time when they interacted with your application, which day of the week they interacted, the day of the month they interacted, most visited user location while interaction, and the type of device used for interaction.

- **Tracking marketing campaign progress using split testing**: You can track which marketing campaign provides the best results and which campaign provides the most conversions and sales.

- **Pointing out ineffective campaigns**: Either update and improve the campaign or remove it.

Setting up an account on Flurry Analytics

Flurry provides you with the analytics features listed earlier. To get started with Flurry Analytics, you need to set up your application on Flurry. The following steps will help you to create and set up your application on Flurry.com:

1. Set up an account at Flurry.com by signing up. Follow the steps listed on the website to do so.

2. After signing up, create and set up your application on Flurry as shown in the following screenshot:

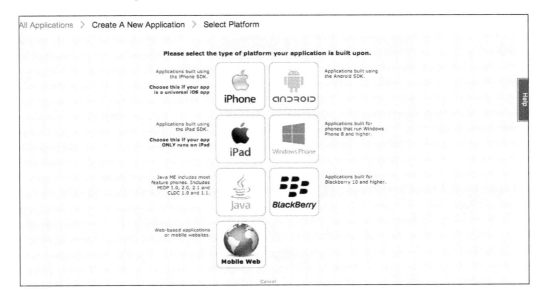

3. Select **iPhone** or **iPad** as your application type and pick an application name and category for the application as shown in the following screenshot:

4. Here you go! You have created the application successfully in Flurry.

5. After registering successfully, you will get a unique application key, which we will use to track the application further in the project.

6. Download the latest Flurry SDK from the link provided after creating the application on Flurry, as shown in the following screenshot:

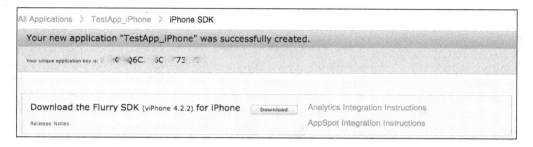

Integrating the library with your project

Click on the download button to download the Flurry SDK for an iPhone. You will get the following files after extracting the downloaded zipped file:

- ProjectApiKey.txt: This file holds the name of your project and your project's API key
- Analytics-README.pdf: This file contains all the instructions to use Flurry
- FlurryAnalytics/FlurryAnalytics.h: This is a header file that contains all the methods that are required for Flurry integration
- FlurryAnalytics/libFlurryAnalytics.a: This is the required library that contains the files related to Flurry's collection along with its reporting code

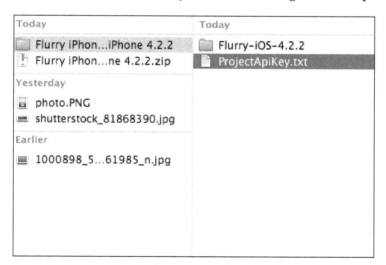

Carry out the following steps to add the Flurry SDK to your project:

1. Launch the finder and drag the `Flurry/` folder in your `Project` file folder. (Note that in case you are upgrading the Flurry SDK, make sure that you remove the existing Flurry folder from the project).

2. Now open your project and add the Flurry files by navigating to **File | Add Files** to <YOUR_PROJECT> to see the following screen:

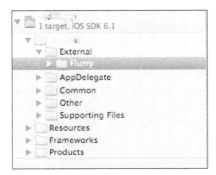

3. After adding Flurry, add the `SystemConfiguration.framework` file in your application. This framework is required for Reachability functions to manage your network-related operations efficiently.

Setting up basic code

To set up Flurry, open your `Application Delegate` file and import Flurry on top, exactly where you imported all the other header files. Then, inside your `applicationDidFinishLaunching:` method, call `[Flurry startSession:@"YOUR_API_KEY"];` with the following code:

```
#import "Flurry.h"
- (void)applicationDidFinishLaunching:(UIApplication *)application {
[Flurry startSession:@"YOUR_API_KEY"];
//your code
}
```

Downloading the example code

You can download the example code files for all Packt books you have purchased from your account at http://www.packtpub.com. If you purchased this book elsewhere, you can visit http://www.packtpub.com/support and register to have the files e-mailed directly to you.

That's it! This is all you need to configure to start receiving the basic updates and metric analytics from Flurry. The basic metrics provide you with all the items under the Usage, Audience, and Technical sections.

This includes tracking all the basic items such as the application's Usage, Audience, and Technical sections in the Flurry portal.

The previous code will allow you to access features that are explained in the following sections.

Sessions

A session can be described as an end user's one-time use of the application. This tracking starts at the application launch and ends when the user forces a close or terminates the application. Flurry allows users to specify the session's start and stop times; however, it depends on the platform. Note that the session does not depend on the number of screens viewed in the application and the amount of time the application is used.

In case your users are using application in the offline mode or when they are offline, Flurry stores the data locally and pushes the data to Flurry the next time your application is open in the online mode. This is so that you do not lose any data.

Active Users

Active Users is defined as the number of users having at least one session in a given period of time, that is, days, weeks, and months. In case a user launches your application more than once, it will still be counted only once. So, for any given time interval, you will have a unique count of the active users.

New Users

When a user first begins to use your application, Flurry refers to this user as a New User. Flurry provides a unique device ID to identify the new users, and these vary depending on the platform. Flurry recognizes new users when they initiate or start using the application. If the user has downloaded the application and has not launched it, it will not be counted. If a user deletes the application and reinstalls it on the same device or upgrades the device to a new version, it will not be re-counted. However, if a user downloads the application to a new device, it will be counted again as the new user count mainly depends on the device identifier.

Session Length

This is defined as the length or duration of the total session. It's basically the time between the application's start event and end event, which may vary based on the platform used. In some cases, such as when the application crashes, we have the start time of the application event, but there is no end time recorded. Hence, the session length is unknown. Flurry does not include instances for the calculation of average and median session length. Session length can vary depending on the way you integrate the SDK in your application project and whether you follow the recommended practices.

Frequency of Use

The number of sessions with respect to unique users over a given period of time is called **Frequency of Use**. Flurry tracks the frequency of use of your application on an individual user basis, so that the aggregated metrics will display the real average value and their estimates.

Benchmarks

Flurry has vast amounts of data. So to ease the reading of useful information, Flurry leverages its data to provide readers with useful benchmarks. You can track your application performance and results by comparing them against category benchmarks on the selected metrics.

Page Views

This section allows you to access the number of the application's discrete sections or screens accessed by users. You can customize and decide the way you want to define page views. We will learn about Page Views in more detail in the upcoming chapters. You can track your screens and check which pages are accessed the most.

User Paths

Flurry allows you to track the paths that users take while navigating through your application. You can track customized events and the user path. Flurry accumulates this data automatically, calculates the final figures, and provides valuable insights that can help you to check the pathways followed by the user while using your application.

Lifecycle Metrics

You can track and access groups and users, and based on the date, you can even measure their retention rates. This includes new users of the application along with the page views.

User Retention

This section crunches your data and provides you with data on the users filtered by cohort. User Retention depends on when the user has launched the application's log with that. It will measure whether they are still in the active user category of the application. This metric contains the retained user that had at least one session with your application in the past seven days from the current date.

Version Adoption

This section helps you to track the number of users that are ported to the new version of the application. It also gives you details about the evolution in usage over a period of time as the user upgrades the software version.

Demographic Estimates

This section details the gender and age of the users using your application. You can check which age group and users are your prominent customers. However, to read this in detail, you need to provide these details to Flurry using its SDK. In case you do not provide such information, Flurry will use its own algorithms to estimate these data sets.

Time of Day Reporting

It tracks the time of the day when your application was used or viewed according to its local time. Hourly reporting allows you to see the usage of your application on an hour-by-hour basis. It provides detailed and important control over the user activity.

Geographic Usage

This section helps you to get reports based on a user's geographical location and further break it down by geographical area in terms of average active users, total sessions, percentage of users retained, and the median session length.

Language Metrics

This section helps you to fetch the number of new users, active users, sessions, and the number of retained users filtered by users, device language. You can get good insight into your application's users based on geographical locations.

Devices

You can read data regarding the device on which the application is used the most. Flurry provides you with the data count for the sessions opened by any specific device type. The data received by Flurry is provided by the manufacturer of the device, but sometimes it is not available in few of the devices. Not all the devices support data sharing on Flurry.

Carriers

This section provides you with the tracked reports of the number of sessions that are opened by users using specific carriers. You can filter the graphs and charts based on the specific carrier's data to get a report on the carrier your application is used on the most. Note that not all sessions and carriers can provide such data.

Firmware Versions

Flurry generates data based on the number of sessions generated by the device's firmware. You access the application's usability based on specific firmware. Note that not all firmware provides such a feature for generating a session's data.

Logging Events

Flurry allows you to log custom events to track user-specific actions made in your application, for example, browsing products, playing the radio, social media sharing, and so on. These activities help you to understand how users interact with your application. The following points will help you to capture the information.

Events

Events can be divided into two levels based on their architecture. The top level in this hierarchy is the specific action, in our case, the playing of music using your application. Let's name this event as *Playing Music*. By tracking such events, you can measure the number of users who read articles from your application along with the frequency of the articles that are read from your application, and so on.

You can use the following code to track such custom events in your application:

```
[Flurry logEvent:@"Article_Read"];
```

Flurry allows you to track a maximum of 300 events for each of your applications. After adding such custom events in your application, Flurry will automatically create user paths based on the event data so you can access the path that the user is following while using your application. You can also create funnels and user segments to track the path followed by a user while using the application.

Event Parameter

Event Parameter is the next stage of the Event structure that we saw in previous topics. Flurry allows you to pass custom event parameters that define the characteristics of the event. For example, a characteristic of the *Playing Music* event is the artist of the album. Characteristics of the user can be their status, such as registered users, guest users, or anonymous users. These parameters will help you to easily filter the graphs and distribution data for the event based on its characteristics. This will help you to know which song is the most played song or which album has has the maximum listeners. This can also provide you with the statistical percentage, for example, you can track the percentage of users that are playing a particular album;

```
NSDictionary *artistParams =
    [NSDictionary dictionaryWithObjectsAndKeys:
      @"John Mayer", @"Artist", // Capture artist info
      @"Registered", @"User_Status", // Capture user status
      nil];

[Flurry logEvent:@"Artist_Played" withParameters:artistParams];
```

Your event can catch a maximum of 10 parameters, and each parameter can hold an infinite number of values that are associated with it. For instance, for our `Artist` parameters, there can be hundreds of possible values for artists who have released albums. You can track all the artists using this one parameter on Flurry.

Event Duration

Flurry provides a way to track your events with time duration and metric access to the average overall length of the event filtered by sessions and users, which are automatically recorded by Flurry based on the usage of the application. To capture the event duration along with the event and associated characteristic parameters, you can use the following log pattern of logging the event duration along with the event parameters:

```objc
NSDictionary *artistParams =
    [NSDictionary dictionaryWithObjectsAndKeys:
     @"John Mayer", @"Artist", // Capture artist info
     @"Registered", @"User_Status", // Capture user status
     nil];

[Flurry logEvent:@"Artist_Played" withParameters:artistParams
  timed:YES];

// In a callback of the function which captures user navigation
  away from artist played.
[Flurry endTimedEvent:@"Artist_Played" withParameters:nil];
// You can pass in additional
//params or update existing ones here as well
```

Segmentation

Flurry allows you to create segments as well. The concept behind segmentation is to divide your users into groups to assess their overall collective behavior. Similarly, you can also get the group's users, which are filtered based on the set of actions they take or the pathways they followed to use the application. This method will help you to create corresponding events to track such users. In the preceding example we discussed, you can browse through the Flurry portal and create a segment or a group to access only the metrics of admin-based users who are playing songs from John Mayer's album. Segments prove to be a powerful tool to locate and rapidly understand the most engaged and valuable users of the application. You will learn segmentation in more detail in the upcoming chapters.

Summary

In this chapter, we explored the requirements of using analytics in mobile application development and Flurry services to track applications and user behavior. We started by exploring the basic needs of analytics in our mobile application. Then, we learned to set up the application on the Flurry portal. Next, we learned the integration of Flurry in our iOS project along with basic setup code. Finally, we saw how to track application events using various methods.

In the next chapter, we will learn about tracking our application in more detail to gather useful data from user activities.

Tracking Applications

2

This chapter explores various ways to track your application using Flurry. This application provides advanced ways to track applications in order to generate useful data. If you want to know which device your application is accessed on the most or know the age group of the users who are using the application the most. In this chapter, we will learn to track the application specifying the parameters that will help us to provide filters for the generated and gathered data.

Also, we will learn about the following in detail:

- Ways to set up goals to track your application
- Tracking time spent by users on the application
- Module-based application tracking
- Tracking specific versions of the application

Settings goals

In the previous chapter, we learnt about setting up and installing Flurry in your project. In this chapter, we will track an application and its specific sections using goals to generate detailed reports. Your goals will vary depending on your requirements for the data you want to gather from your application. So Flurry provides you with a way to track all your events using your event ID.

You can use the following code to track the event:

```
[Flurry logEvent:@"EVENT_NAME"];
```

The `logEvent:` method logs your event every time it's triggered during the application session. This method helps you to track how often that event is triggered. You can track up to 300 different event IDs. However, the length of each event ID should be less than 255 characters.

After the event is triggered, you can track that event from your Flurry dashboard. As is explained in the following screenshot, your events will be listed in the **Events** section. After clicking on **Event Summary**, you can see a list of the events you have created along with the statistics of the generated data as shown in the following screenshot:

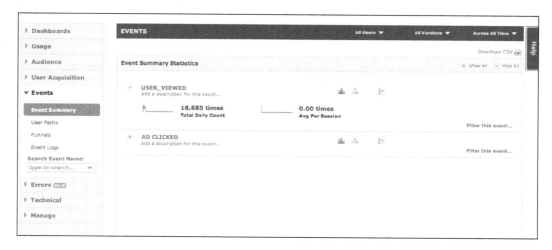

You can fetch the detailed data by clicking on the event name (for example, **USER_ VIEWED**). This section will provide you with a chart-based analysis of the data as shown in the following screenshot:

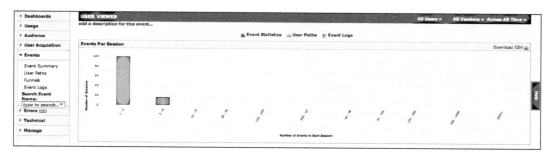

The **Events Per Session** chart will provide you with details about how frequently a particular event is triggered in a session.

Other than this, you are provided with the following data charts as well:

- **Unique Users Performing Event**: This chart will explain the frequency of unique users triggering the event.

- **Total Events**: This chart holds the event-generation frequency over a time period. You can access the frequency of the event being triggered over any particular time slot.
- **Average Events Per Session**: This charts holds the average frequency of the events that happen per session.

There is another variation of this method, as shown in the following code, which allows you to track the events along with the specific user data provided:

```
[Flurry logEvent:@"EVENT_NAME" withParameters:YOUR_NSDictionary];
```

This version of the `logEvent:` method counts the frequency of the event and records dynamic parameters in the form of dictionaries. External parameters should be in the `NSDictionary` format, whereas both the key and the value should be in the `NSString` object format. Let's say you want to track how frequently your comment section is used and see the comments, then you can use this method to track such events along with the parameters. You can track up to 300 different events with an event ID length less than 255 characters. You can provide a maximum of 10 event parameters per event.

The following example illustrates the use of the `logEvent:` method along with optional parameters in the dictionary format:

```
NSDictionary *dictionary =
  [NSDictionary dictionaryWithObjectsAndKeys:@"your dynamic
  parameter value",
  @"your dynamic parameter name",
  nil];
[Flurry logEvent:@"EVENT_NAME" withParameters:dictionary];
```

In case you want Flurry to log all your application sections/screens automatically, then you should pass `navigationController` or as a parameter to count all your pages automatically using one of the following code:

```
[Flurry logAllPageViews:navigationController];
[Flurry logAllPageViews:tabBarController];
```

The Flurry SDK will create a delegate on your `navigationController` or `tabBarController` object, whichever is provided to detect the page's navigation. Each navigation detected will be tracked by the Flurry SDK automatically as a page view. You only need to pass each object to the Flurry SDK once. However you can pass multiple instances of different navigation and tab bar controllers.

There can be some cases where you can have a view controller that is not associated with any navigation or tab bar controller. Then you can use the following code:

```
[Flurry logPageView];
```

The preceding code will track the event independently of navigation and tab bar controllers. For each user interaction you can manually log events.

Tracking time spent

Flurry allows you to track events based on the duration factor as well. You can use the `[Flurry logEvent: timed:]` method to log your event in time as shown in the following code:

```
[Flurry logEvent:@"EVENT_NAME" timed:YES];
```

In case you want to pass additional parameters along with the event name, you can use the following type of the `logEvent:` method to start a timed event for event `Parameters` as shown in the following code:

```
[Flurry logEvent:@"EVENT_NAME" withParameters:YOUR_NSDictionary
   timed:YES];
```

The aforementioned method can help you to track your timed event along with the dynamic data provided in the dictionary format.

You can end all your timed events before the application exits. This can even be accomplished by updating the event with event `Parameters`. If you want to end your events without updating the parameters, you can pass `nil` as the parameters.

If you do not end your events, they will automatically end when the application exits as shown in the following code:

```
[Flurry endTimedEvent:@"EVENT_NAME"
   withParameters:YOUR_NSDictionary];
```

Let's take the following example in which you want to log an event whenever a user comments on any article in your application:

```
NSDictionary *commentParams =
   [NSDictionary dictionaryWithObjectsAndKeys:
   @"User_Comment", @"Comment", // Capture comment info
   @"Registered", @"User_Status", // Capture user status
   nil];
```

```
[Flurry logEvent:@"User_Comment" withParameters:commentParams
  timed:YES];

// In a function that captures when a user post the comment
[Flurry endTimedEvent:@"Article_Read" withParameters:nil];
//You can pass in additional
//params or update existing ones here as well
```

The aforementioned piece of code will help you to log a timed event every time a user comments on a picture in your application. While tracking the event, you are also tracking the comment and the user registered by specifying them in the dictionary.

Tracking errors

Flurry provides you with a method to track errors as well. You can use the following methods to track errors on Flurry:

```
[Flurry logError:@"ERROR_NAME" message:@"ERROR_MESSAGE"
  exception:e];
```

You can track exceptions and errors that occurred in the application by providing the name of the error (ERROR_NAME) along with the messages, such as ERROR_MESSAGE, with an exception object. Flurry reports the first ten errors in each session.

You can fetch all the application exceptions and specifically uncaught exceptions on Flurry. You can use the logError:message:exception: class method to catch all the uncaught exceptions. These exceptions will be logged in Flurry in the **Error** section, which is accessible on the Flurry dashboard:

```
// Uncaught Exception Handler - sent through Flurry.
void uncaughtExceptionHandler(NSException *exception) {
  [Flurry logError:@"Uncaught"
    message:@"Crash" exception:exception];
}

- (void)applicationDidFinishLaunching:(UIApplication *)application
 {
 NSSetUncaughtExceptionHandler(&uncaughtExceptionHandler);
 [Flurry startSession:@"YOUR_API_KEY"];
 // ....
 }
```

Flurry also helps you to catch all the uncaught exceptions generated by the application. All the exceptions will be caught by using the `NSSetUncaughtExceptionHandler` method in which you can pass a method that will catch all the exceptions raised during the application session.

All the errors reported can also be tracked using the `logError:message:error:` method. You can pass the error name, message, and object to log the `NSError` error on Flurry as shown in the following code:

```
    - (void) webView:(UIWebView *)webView
      didFailLoadWithError:(NSError *)error
{
  [Flurry logError:@"WebView No Load"
    message:[error localizedDescription] error:error];
}
```

Tracking versions

When you develop applications for mobile devices, it's obvious that you will evolve your application at every stage, pushing the latest updates for the application, which creates a new version of the application on the application store. To track the application based on these versions, you need to set up the Flurry to track your application versions as well. This can be done using the following code:

```
[Flurry setAppVersion:App_Version_Number];
```

So by using the aforementioned method, you can track your application based on its version. For example, if you have released an application and unfortunately it's having a critical bug, then you can track your application based on the current version and the errors that are tracked by Flurry from the application.

You can access data generated from Flurry's **Dashboards** by navigating to **Flurry Classic**. This will, by default, load a time-based graph of the application session for all versions. However, you can access the user session graph by selecting a version from the drop-down list as shown in the following screenshot:

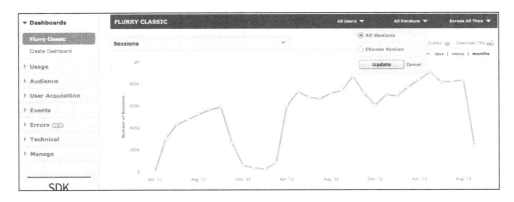

This is how the drop-down list will appear. Select a version and click on **Update** as shown in the following screenshot:

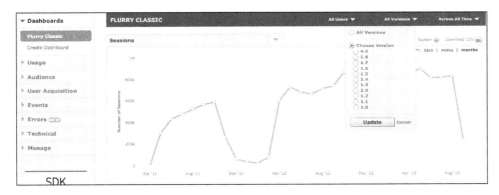

The previous action will generate a version-based graph for a user's session with the as number of times users have opened the app in the given time frame shown in the following screenshot:

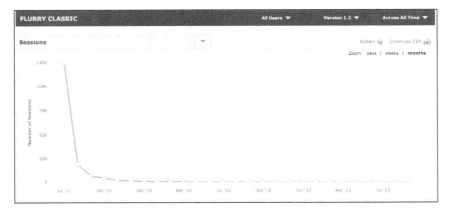

Along with that, Flurry also provides user retention graphs to gauge the number of users and the usage of application over a period of time.

User details

Flurry provides many methods to track users based on their information. For example, if you need to track the user based on their ID, you can use the following code:

```
[Flurry setUserID:@"USER_ID"];
```

Note that as per the terms of service, you are not allowed to pass the **Unique Device ID (UDID)** of the device as a parameter in this method.

After identifying the user based on their ID, you can use the following method to track their age (the input parameter should be greater than 0).

```
[Flurry setAge:23];
```

After tracking the user's age, you can access the data generated by Flurry to analyze the age group of the users who use the application the most, as shown in the following screenshot:

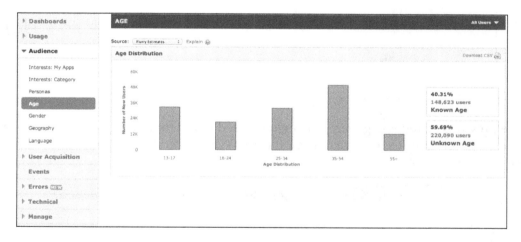

To identify the gender of the user, you can use the following method:

```
[Flurry setGender:@"m"];
```

The preceding code takes either m for male or f for female to specify the gender. After tracking the user's gender through the application, you can access the application's generated data through Flurry. You can navigate through **Audience** and click on **Gender** to access the chart based on the data for users, gender as shown in the following screenshot:

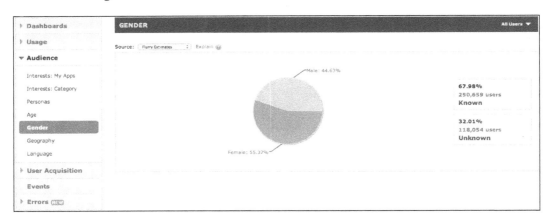

As shown in the preceding chart, you can track the percentage of male or female users of your application along with the percentage of unspecified gender users.

Location tracking

You can fetch the user's location by using the CCLocationManager class. The following code will start to get the current location of the user. However, to track a user's location, you need to add CoreLocation.framework in your project to track the location of a user in Flurry as shown:

```
CLLocationManager *locationManager =
  [[CLLocationManager alloc] init];
[locationManager startUpdatingLocation];
```

After getting the location, you can set the location in Flurry. You can set CCLocationManagerDelegate to get the callback when the updated location is received. Once the updated location is received from the locationManager class, you can use the following method to set the same on Flurry:

```
CLLocation *location = locationManager.location;
[Flurry setLatitude:location.coordinate.latitude
        longitude:location.coordinate.longitude
        horizontalAccuracy:location.horizontalAccuracy
        verticalAccuracy:location.verticalAccuracy];
```

The preceding method will update the user's current GPS location on Flurry. It will only save the last location information. Tracking the location will help you to track the user's location over the map in Flurry's statistics. These maps will help you to check where users are accessing your application from, as shown in the following screenshot:

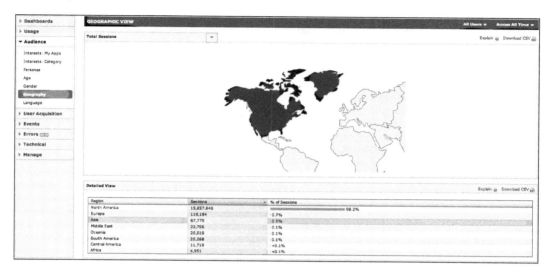

After setting the data through your application, you can access the data gathered through Flurry. Navigate to **Audience**, then click on **Geography** to access the data chart for the location where the application is used the most. The maps in the first section provide a brief pictorial representation of the data. If you want to access the detailed data, you can access it through the **Detailed View** section.

 Note that Apple will reject your application submission if your application is not using location services in a meaningful way.

Controlling data

You can control your data submission on Flurry using various methods provided by them. The following method allows Flurry to send session data when the application is closed or when the application is started:

```
[Flurry setSessionReportsOnCloseEnabled:
    (BOOL)sendSessionReportsOnClose];
```

This method is set to YES by default and will improve the speed at which your application analytics data is updated on Flurry. It will prolong the termination process of the application because of network latency:

```
[Flurry setSessionReportsOnPauseEnabled:
```

This method is also set to the YES option by default. When this function is set as YES, Flurry will try to send the data when the application is in the pause mode. Normally when the application is started, Flurry will try to send the data generated. This is will improve the speed of updating data on Flurry.

```
[Flurry setSecureTransportEnabled:
    (BOOL)secureTransport];
```

The preceding method is used to transport your data securely to Flurry. This method will encrypt your data through SSL and send to Flurry in an encrypted form. The Flurry SDK will attempt to send the data when it's in the pause mode. This option is disabled by default, thus holds NO as its BOOL value. This will prolong the pause process of the application because of network latency from SSL secure handshaking and encryption.

Summary

In this chapter, we explored the ways to track the application on Flurry and to gather meaningful data on Flurry. We started by setting goals to track the application. Then we learned how to track the time spent by users on the application along using user data tracking. Then we learned location-based tracking to track the application usage based on location. Finally, we learned how to control the data generated by the Flurry application.

In the next chapter, we will learn about the ways to analyze the data generated by Flurry.

3
Data Analysis

In this chapter, we will see how Flurry helps you to analyze data. It provides you with unique insights into your application and uses its huge data collection to help you with your analysis.

We will learn about the following features of Flurry that help with data analysis and how to use them:

- Funnel analysis
- Segments
- Portfolio Analytics
- User Acquisition analysis
- Customizing your dashboard
- Crash Analytics
- Big Data benefit

Funnel analysis

You can select a sequence of events from your application to form a funnel. This will define how users use your application, let you define the path to be tracked, and when users can traverse that path in your application. Now Flurry will display the statistics specific to that sequence. For example, you can create a series of events where a user signs in to your application, selects a particular product, views its features, adds it to the cart, and confirms the order. In this way, you can understand the percentage of consumers who move from one step to the next. You can then find out where event transition improvement is needed or applaud the winning transition.

 It takes one day to propagate all your data to Flurry.

To create a funnel, go to the left-hand side bar, click on **Funnels** in the **Events** drop-down, and select **Add new funnels**. As shown in the following screenshot, you can continue here with the name and description of your funnel:

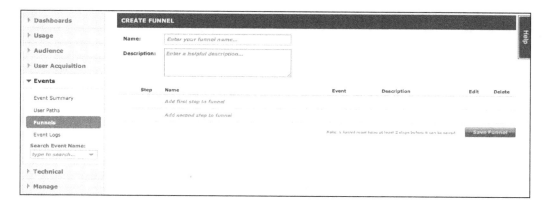

You will see the interface shown in following screenshot while adding each step to edit the funnel:

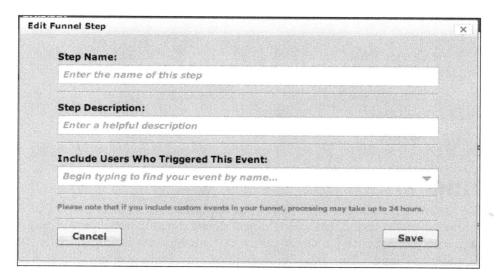

As we can see in the preceding screenshot, you can name and describe each step while adding it to the funnel. You can also include the users who triggered this event if you need to. Here, all the events present in the **Events** tab will be listed as drop-down options for your selection as a step in the funnel.

The advantage here is that you don't need to predict the steps in the funnel. You can select them from the list of **Events** at any time to form a funnel.

The following screenshot demonstrate the editing of a funnel. You can select events from the event drop-down list:

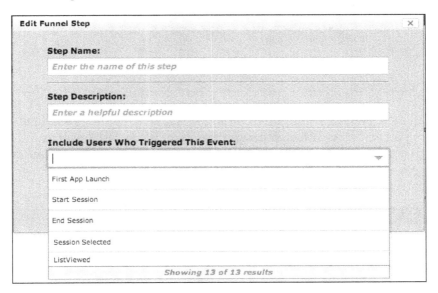

Segments

Segments are basically different categories of application users who represent a group. We can create segments that will help us to monitor a finely tuned group of typical users. For example, you can create a segment of users who are adults, a segment of users who are male, a segment of user who are female, and so on.

The parameters for segmentation can include the following:

1. Date range
2. Custom events
3. Usage
4. Location
5. User gender
6. User age range
7. User language

To create segments, go to the **Manage** tab on the left-hand side bar and click on the **Segments** item in its drop-down list.

You will find the **Create New Segment** button as show in the following screenshot:

Clicking on the **Create New Segment** button will take you to the parameter setting page. Here you can set up the date range criteria, usage criteria, user/audience specific criteria, location criteria, and name your segment from the **Date Range**, **Usage**, **Custom Events**, **Audience**, and **Location** tabs respectively as shown in the following screenshot:

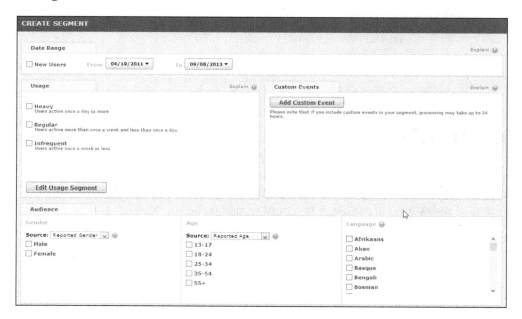

You can even select a certain location or region to be included in your segment. The following screenshot demonstrates how to do so:

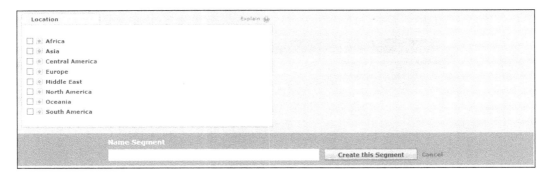

Once a segment is created, you cannot edit it. You'd have to delete it and create a new segment. For every segment created, you can see every metric for an application. There will also be a segment drop-down where you can view and select the segment you have created.

Portfolio Analytics

A certain organization can track more than one application with Portfolio Analytics using Flurry. For such cases, there can exist a portfolio of applications configured in Flurry for analysis. Now with Flurry, you can track the conversion between one or more of your applications. For example, we may be advertising one of our applications in any of our other applications; thus, users may be sourced from one of your applications to another. An analysis of these patterns can be very useful.

Through portfolio analysis, you can get metrics for the following:

1. **Cross-Selling**: One of your applications refers users to another of your applications
2. **Up-Selling**: One of your applications is upgraded to "paid", that is, free-to-paid conversion
3. **Cross-App Usage**: Users using several applications within one portfolio
4. **Cross-App Funnels**: Users sharing funnels between several applications

To set up Cross-Selling tracking, go to the **Conversions** tab on the left side bar and click on the **Cross-Selling** item in the drop-down.

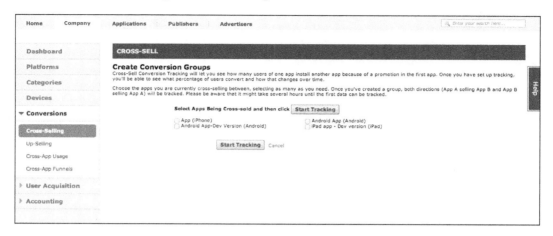

Here we will find all the applications in the portfolio listed for our selection. Select the applications as per your need and click on the **Start Tracking** button as shown in the preceding screenshot.

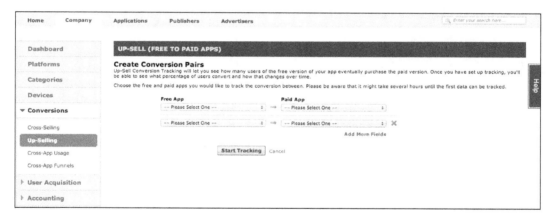

To track Cross-App usage, go to the **Conversions** tab on the left side bar and click on **Cross-App Usage** in the drop-down. Here it will show you the tabular representation of data for users who are in common between two applications in each row, as shown in the following screenshot:

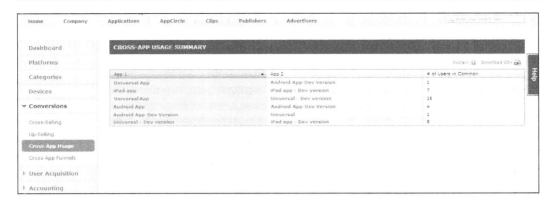

CROSS-APP funnel will help you to track several applications; it helps you to create a funnel common to several applications in one portfolio. Creating a CROSS-APP funnel includes defining a series of steps between applications, which leads to conversions.

To create CROSS-APP funnels, go to the **Conversions** tab on the left side bar and click on **Cross-App Funnels** in the drop-down. You can start adding funnels by clicking on the **Add new funnel** button shown in the following screenshot:

When we click on the **Add new funnel** button, we are redirected to the basic interface for creating a funnel, just as we discussed earlier in this chapter while going through the process of creating funnel. Here you can name and describe the Cross-App funnel that is being created and add steps to it.

 It takes one day to propagate all your generated data over to Flurry.

While adding the steps in the pop-up box, you can name and describe the step. You can also select which application listed will track users and the required events (in the last row) as shown in the following screenshot:

User Acquisition analysis

User Acquisition helps you to track your users' engagement-related statistics. This section of Flurry helps you to track your user engagement through several factors based on channel, clicks, installations, and many more.

User Acquisition analysis can be done on a complete portfolio of applications as well as on a single application being tracked in Flurry.

You can target your campaign as well as your channels to get quantifiable data, which can help you to know your quality users around the globe.

This analysis is the best way to know the return on investment in marketing. We can invest in various marketing channels, such as mobile ad networks or web mobile e-mail campaigns. Flurry User Acquisition analytics provides you with metrics to quantify the quality of acquired users, a pictorial representation of data, and their spending pattern on the basis of user interaction with your application.

The reports from this analysis can help you tell which advertising deal is going to be a good deal for you and provide you with quality users who will help generate good revenue. You are able to compare several of your marketing sources on the basis of various criterion such as geographical location, gender, age, and retention rate.

You can track your installations and quality of installations using this **User Acquisition** section. Flurry uses segments and funnels to measure the quality of installations. Using the campaign section, you can track user installations based on your custom funnels and segments. We can create a campaign by navigating through the **User Acquisition** tab on the left side bar and selecting **Create Campaign** as shown in the following screenshot:

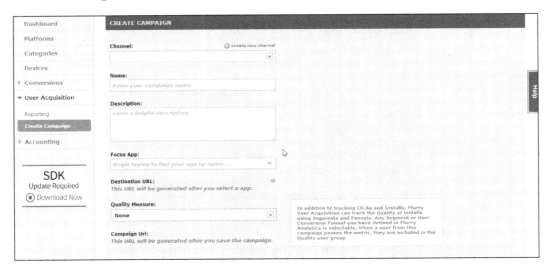

Here you can select all the global channels from the drop-down that appears from the **Channel** text box. In the **Quality Measure** drop-down, we can select **Funnel** or **Segment**. In the **User Acquisition** drop-down, you will see the **Reporting** tab where you can find reports for the same as shown in the following screenshot:

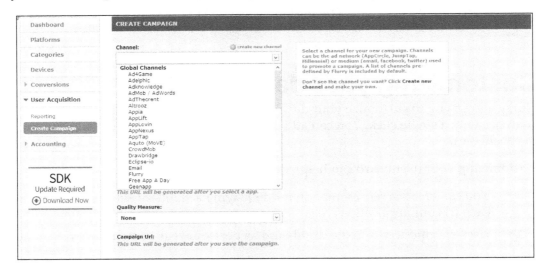

After selecting the channel, you have to provide the name and other details for creating the campaign as shown in the following screenshot:

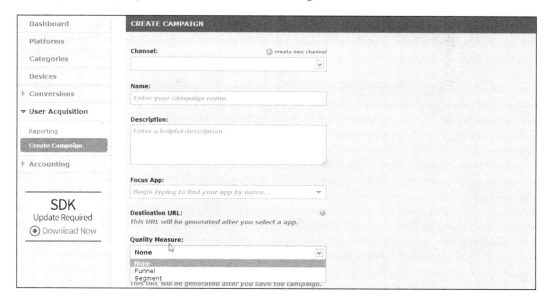

Flurry allows you to create Custom Quality metrics according to the requirements of the implementer. Along with this, Flurry also creates Standard Quality metrics, which allow you to track some standard events.

 Please note that to implement User Requisition Analytics in your application, you will require **Flurry Analytics SDK**. It is currently available for the iOS and Android platforms. Flurry currently supports only Ad the Networks, Mobile Web, and E-mail channels.

Customizing your dashboard

Flurry allows you to customize your dashboard to get all your details and data analytics with a single click. You can add all your frequently accessed components in the dashboard.

Customizing your dashboard can help you in the following ways:

- You can create a representation for displaying a standard set of metrics for each of your applications
- User-specific access to the dashboard as per your requirements

- You can set up an application-specific dashboard
- You can select the most frequently used applications for quick access

To create a custom dashboard, go to the **Create Dashboard** item on the **Dashboards** menu item on the left side bar as shown in the following screenshot:

Here you can proceed in two ways:

- By selecting the template provided by Flurry
- By creating your own dashboard from scratch

When creating your own dashboard from scratch, you will get blank widgets. Here you can configure, move, or delete the widgets as per your requirements:

On clicking on the configuration option (the pen icon) in the top-right corner of the widget, it will provide a pop-up with the configuration options.

As shown in the following figure, these configurations are on the basis of the following areas of interest

1. **Usage**
2. **Audience**
3. **Events**
4. **Technical**

The following screenshot shows the configuration screen of the widget:

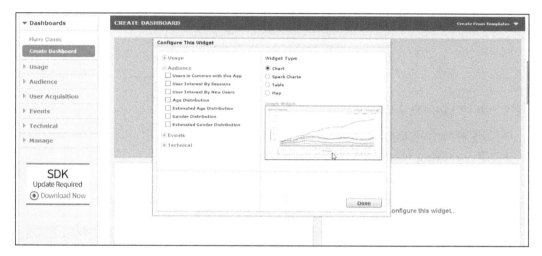

Crash Analytics

Last but not the least, crash analysis can be done by the **Errors** item in the **Technical** menu item on the side bar in any application page. It gives you a graphical representation of the total errors over time, average errors per session, a detailed view, and exception log. It makes the life of a technical team very easy by helping track mishaps in the application.

The following are the advantages of Crash Analytics in Flurry:

* We can prioritize the errors and crashes that have been tracked. We can do this using the same SDK
* We can receive an e-mail notification of the crash so that the implementers are notified of the application crash before it's too late
* We can get full stack traces of errors with symbolication
* We can find errors listed by their name

We will be learning about Crash Analytics in detail in *Chapter 4*, *Technical Analytics*.

Big Data benefits

Using Flurry gives you the greatest of all the benefits, in the form of Big Data analysis reports. As we all know, Flurry reaches one billion devices per month, and as a result, they are sourced with 3 terabytes of data per day approximately. Similarly, the developers are able to gather information from 3.5 billion sessions per day and are working with 115,000 companies.

So, what does this mean for us? It gives us insights from huge amounts of data, which helps us in the following ways:

- It helps you to set a benchmark from the real world
- You can classify your application into certain categories
- It gives you a demographic estimation of the age and gender of your application users
- Knowing Consumer expectation and point of interest in your application

Summary

In this chapter, we learned about how we can use Flurry to generate metrics according to our needs. We are now familiar with how Flurry can be set up to get a finely tuned analysis of our application data. We now know about the different ways to analyze data related to our application. We learned to create funnels and segments, which are fundamental concepts to fine-tune data analysis.

In the next chapter, we will learn about the ways to track errors using Flurry.

4
Technical Analytics

In this chapter, we will explore various ways to track your application errors in Flurry. Flurry provides advanced methods to track errors in order to enhance the stability of the application in case you want to know the details of the crash, such as the device on which your application crashes the most or the iOS version of the group of users who are facing similar issues. In this chapter, we will learn to track crashes and errors that occur in an application . We will also specify the parameters that will help to provide filters for the data that is generated and gathered. Filtering the data that is gathered will be useful to track and stabilize your application.

Tracking your crashes

It's obvious that applications crash wildly when used even after exhaustive testing. Flurry helps you to investigate your crashes with very specific details that bring down the fixing time for developers. Flurry provides you with details such as the version number, device details, location, and exceptions.

Flurry supports Crash Analytics and offers the following advantages:

- It easily tracks when your application crashes
- It reports nonfatal errors that do not cause crashes
- It provides unique names for specific errors and exceptions

Flurry produces good crash reporting results by resymbolicating crash reports from a device; this whole process is executed on the client side. You have to provide the desymbolication file to resymbolicate the crash reports generated by Flurry.

Crash Analytics is included from iOS 4.2 onwards, so make sure that you are using the latest SDK in your project.

Crash Analytics is disabled by default; you can enable it by using the following code to report the crash:

```
[Flurry setCrashReportingEnabled:YES];
```

By calling the preceding method, you are enabling the crash reporting feature in Flurry.

You can access all your data that is generated over from Flurry. The reports will help you to track all your crashes and identify the root cause of the issue(s). The crash detail report will look similar to the following screenshot when accessed from the Flurry dashboard:

CRASHES			All Firmwares ▼	All Devices ▼	Version 2.2 ▼	Across All Time ▼

New Crashes   Explain 🔍   Download CSV 📥

First Seen	Last Seen	Crashes	Version First Seen	Version Last Seen	Unique Users	
Mar 14, 2013 11:30 AM	Apr 16, 2013 06:03 AM	<redacted> + 162	2.1	2.2	35	
Feb 15, 2013 07:40 AM	Apr 16, 2013 06:23 AM	_objc_msgSend + 15	2.1	2.2	31	
Mar 14, 2013 01:35 PM	Apr 16, 2013 05:37 AM	<redacted> + 162	2.1	2.2	18	
Mar 14, 2013 01:53 PM	Apr 16, 2013 09:14 AM	___exceptionPreprocess + 162	2.1	2.2	12	
Apr 09, 2013 11:06 PM	Apr 16, 2013 03:22 AM	0x396f0000 + 70480	2.2	2.2	10	
Mar 21, 2013 12:40 PM	Apr 16, 2013 07:54 AM	-[NSException encodeWithCoder:] + 218	2.1	2.2	10	

The preceding screenshot lists all the crashes that happen in a session of the application cycle. You can track these crashes based on type. The previous reports and statistics can help to investigate which issue/error is causing the crash, on which firmware version it started, and which version is last seen.

You can even filter your data reporting based on the application version and the devices used. This will help developers to close in on the specific version and device to test the scenario in order to fix the issue, as shown in the following screenshot:

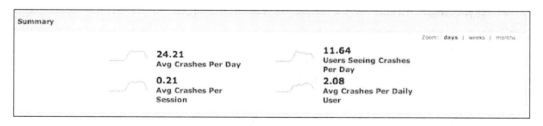

As we just saw, Flurry provides an overall summary of the application status and summarizes a report on the application crashes. This gives you a picture of the stability of the application on the market along with the following details as well:

- **Avg Crashes Per Day**: This provides you with the average number of crashes that occur on a daily basis
- **Users Seeing Crashes Per Day**: This data shows the number of users facing the same type of error in the application on a per-day basis
- **Avg Crashes Per Session**: This data metric will show the average crashes that occur in a particular session
- **Avg Crashes Per Daily User**: This data metric shows the average crashes that occur daily for a particular user

You can access the distribution of the total crashes based on the dates of the crashes. The charts and data are accessible in Flurry as seen in the following screenshot:

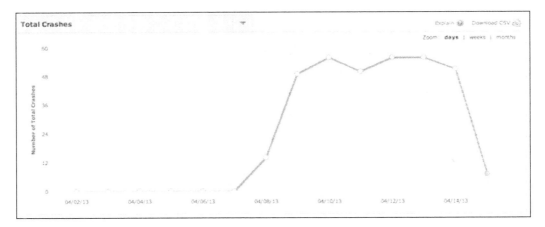

Stack traces

Flurry provides you with a full view of the stack trace. To generate the stack trace, navigate to **Stack Traces** and then to the **Overview** section. Then click on the crash to generate the trace for it. Flurry also provides you with the access to download the full crash report from the same page. If the stack traces are desymbolicated, then Flurry provides you with the option to upload your .dSYM file in iOS to symbolicate the crash report.

The `.dSYM` upload allows developers to upload their application symbolication file automatically to symbolicate the Flurry-generated crash logs, as shown in the following screenshot:

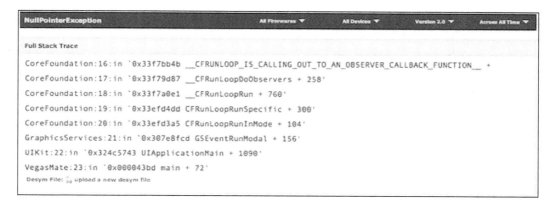

To access the `.dSYM` file of your application, follow these steps:

1. Open your Xcode and then click on **Organizer**.
2. Navigate to your **Archives** tab.
3. Select your application for which you need the `.dSYM` file.
4. Right-click on the application, and then from the menu, click on **Show in Finder**.
5. This will open the finder window that your application archive is placed on.
6. Right-click on the application archive in your **Finder** window, and from the menu, click on **Show Package Contents**.

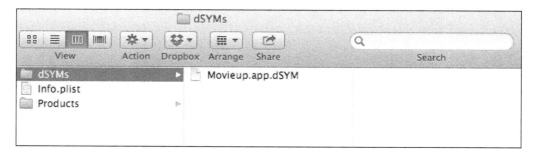

7. Just select this .dSYM file (as shown in the following screenshot) and upload it to Flurry to generate symbolication for your crash.

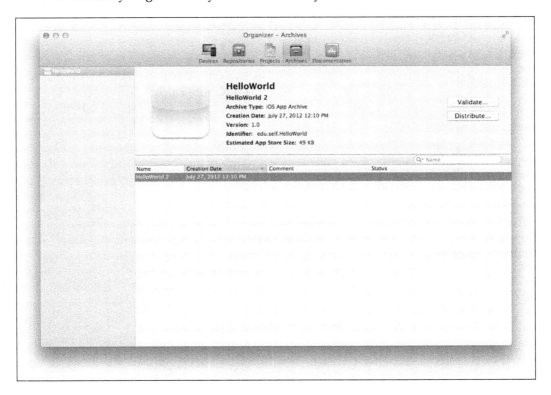

To upload .dSYM, you need to follow the procedure given in the following section.

Uploading dSYM

You need to use the HTTP POST request to upload your dSYM file to Flurry. You can fetch your dSYM file from Xcode. To upload the dSYM file, you need to compress it into tar + gzip or zip formats as Flurry currently supports these formats. gzip is recommended to speed up the uploading process.

You need to execute the following command to upload your dSYM:

```
curl -F "content=@DSYMFILE"
  "http://api.flurry.com/dsym/upload?apiAccessCode=
  APIACCESSCODE&apiKey=APIKEY&versionName=VERSIONNAME"
```

The parameter description is given as follows:

- APIACCESSCODE: Replace this with the unique code provided to you by the Flurry API. You can access this code by navigating to the **Manage** link on the Flurry website in the top center.

- APIKEY: Replace this with the unique code for your application. Flurry provides a unique APIKEY, for all applications. To access your application's unique APIKEY open the Flurry site and navigate to your application by clicking on your **Application Name**. Then click on the **Manage** tab in the bottom-left corner of the page.

- VERSIONNAME: This is the version name of the application that you are uploading the dSYM for. The version name should match the version string of your project from Xcode DSYM:. This is the file that you need to upload to Flurry for symbolication.

After executing the command, your dSYM file will start uploading to Flurry. This can either result in success or failure. Both response formats are discussed in the upcoming section.

Response format

After the execution of the command in the preceding section, you will get a response in either XML or JSON format. If you receive the response code 200, this means the request is fine as HTTP response code 200 signifies a valid request format. It will have content similar to the following code snippet:

```
<success>
<message>Deleted past mapping file for this version</message>
</success>
```

Error codes

If execution fails because of system-related reasons or because there is something wrong with the request, you will receive an error response instead of a success response. You will receive a HTTP response code other than 200 along with a message that describes the reason for the error as shown in the following code snippet:

```
<error>
  <code>100</code>
  <message>API Key not found</message>
</error>
```

You can reach out to Flurry in case you are not able to debug or troubleshoot the reason behind the error message.

Tracking errors

Flurry provides you with complete access to trace your application's technical data generated by Flurry. This data helps to simplify the decision-making process. Let's say you need to decide which versions of iOS you should support for your application; in that case, you need Flurry to help you crunch the data and let you know the percentage of users that are using which versions of iOS. If you want to drop support for iOS 4.3 from your application, you can access the percentage of users using the application on that particular OS version and make a decision.

To access this data, navigate to the **Technical** section from your left-hand panel. This will generate the following statistics:

- **Top Devices Model**: This statistic provides a detailed insight into your application's user base on each device available, as shown in the following screenshot:

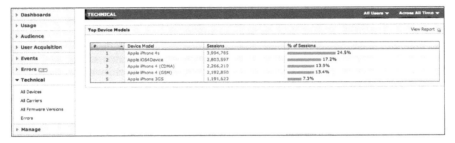

You can even access the data that corresponds to each device; just click on the model of the device you need to explore in detail. Let's say you need to explore the details of an iPhone 4S device; just click on that option to access the details on it:

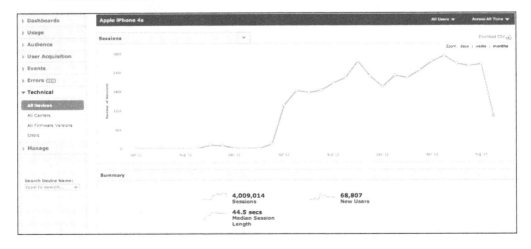

- **Top Carriers**: This provides detailed information about the user's phone carrier, which used by the application, along with the number of sessions that are used on the particular carrier.

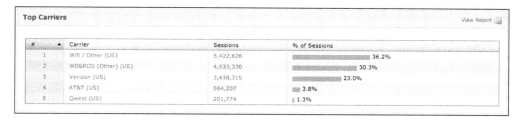

- **Top Firmware Versions**: This provides detailed statistics about the firmware versions that the application is used on along with the number of sessions on that firmware.

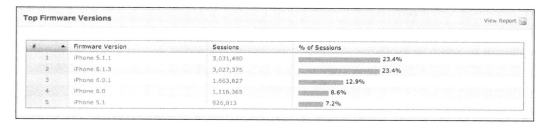

The preceding statistics will help you to improve the decision-making process. Now you can analyze the data and on that basis, you can decide which framework you should target and what the user's retention is based on the firmware.

To access the errors, you need to navigate to the **Technical** section and then click on **Errors** to access the list of error statistics. This will generate the following types of specifications for you:

- **Total Errors**: This graph will provide you with an overview of the total number of errors that occur in all sessions. The graph will be as shown in the following screenshot:

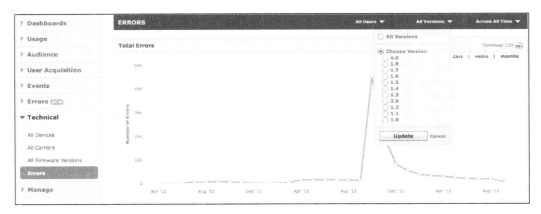

- **Avg Errors Per Session**: This provides you with time-based data to track the average number of errors per session:

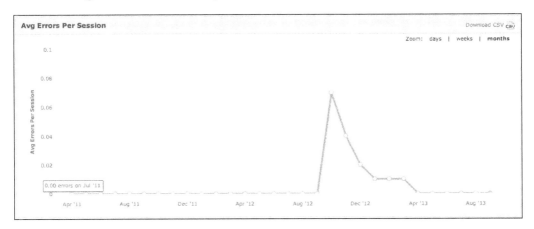

- **Errors Per Session**: This graph shows you the number of errors that occur in each session. The closer the bar is to the left-hand side, the stable more the application is:

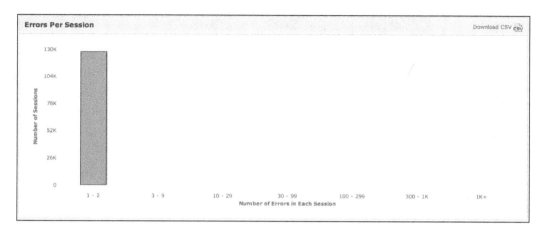

- **Detailed View**: This shows you the number of errors that occur in the sessions. So, in the example shown in the following screenshot, no error has occurred in most of the sessions, while only one or two errors occurred in 0.8 percent of sessions:

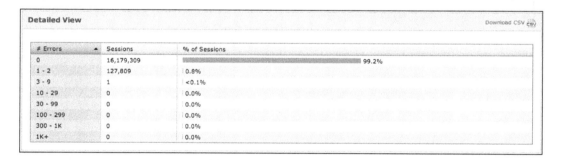

- **Exception Log**: If you are using try-catch statements to add stability to your code, you can access all your exception logs on Flurry. Other than that, all the exceptions will be logged and you can access that gathered information using the statistics available:

Exception Log   Download CSV 📥

Page 1		next »

Timestamp ▼	Error	Details
09/12/13 22:04:03 IST (2)	NSRangeException: Cannot remove an observer <UAUser 0x1d5b8a70> for the key path "deviceToken" from <UAPush 0x1e1c29e0> because it is not registered as an observer. Msg: Crash	V: 2.2.7 P: iPhone E: Uncaught
09/12/13 21:12:08 IST (2)	NSInvalidArgumentException: -[UIImage count]: unrecognized selector sent to instance 0x1e149030 Msg: Crash	V: 2.2.7 P: iPhone E: Uncaught
09/12/13 21:10:36 IST (2)	NSRangeException: Cannot remove an observer <UAUser 0x14e28fd0> for the key path "deviceToken" from <UAPush 0x14e3f730> because it is not registered as an observer. Msg: Crash	V: 2.2.7 P: iPhone E: Uncaught
09/12/13 20:35:11 IST (2)	NSUnknownKeyException: [<BuyInformation 0x60ed280> setValue:forUndefinedKey:]: this class is not key value coding-compliant for the key formatted. Msg: Crash	V: 2.2.2 P: iPhone E: Uncaught

Page 1   next »
Details: V - Version, P - Platform, E - Error ID, M - Method

This includes the time that the exception is being raised at, along with the device information and error description. These exceptions will help you to track the root cause of the bug. As in the preceding example, the exception is thrown by the `NSInvalidArgumentException:` method, which occurs because of an unrecognized selector called on the `UIImage` class. You can target the places where you have called count on the `UIImage` class. In this way, you can target and fix the issues to stabilize your application on the market.

In the same way, if you focus on the next exception that is thrown, you can see that the issue is caused because of the `UAUser` class. This class is of **Urban Airship** for push notifications. So, you can find the location in your code where we registered the user through Urban Airship and track the place where the application has crashed.

In the same way, you can access the description of all the exceptions thrown by the application during the session. You can search for the exception reason in your code base to hammer out the cause of exception or error. This approach will add to the performance of the application.

All the preceding graphs and statistics can be further refined by using the following filters:

- **Users**: This filter helps you refine your data specific to any custom defined segment. You can also create your own segments from here. By default, the statistics shown are for all the users.

- **Versions**: This filter refines your results based on the application version. Let's say you want to find the frequency of errors that occur in the latest version of your application. In such cases, you can use this filter to generate the data for a specific version. By default, it shows data for all available versions.

- **Time**: This filter refines your result based on the time. In case you want to access the data for a particular time slot, you can use this filter to define your custom time slot. This also provides predefined time slots, such as **Last Week** and **Last Month**. By default, it shows statistics and graphs for **All Time**.

Summary

In this chapter, we learned about the ways to track our application crashes and errors in order to provide stability to the application. We started by tracking our application's crashes on Flurry. Then we learned the ways to extract meaningful information from the crash logs to fix the root cause of the crash. Finally, we learned the ways to track our application's errors and exceptions. This type of errors and exception tracking lets us know which files to eliminate and helps gather the important information for developers work on to move towards stabilizing our application's.

In the next chapter, we will learn about the features of Flurry and the ways to use data for different purposes.

5
Using Your Data

In this chapter, we will see how the insights provided by Flurry are useful to us and how we can apply them in different scenarios.

We will learn about the following in detail:

- The ways to measure user quality
- Details about user acquisition, retention, and engagement

Measuring user quality

User Acquisition Analytics in Flurry gives you the ability to analyze the quality of users with respect to your business parameters.

There are various reasons for using Flurry to measure user quality, which are as follows:

- To know which age group is using your application more. We can identify the group that is most engaged with our application. This group is a high-quality group for our application business.
- To know which user age group is contributing more in revenue generation. We can focus on such a user group and monetize them.
- To determine which user age group will be the target for advertisements. Using this, the management can focus on these user groups to maximize the advertisement hit count and interaction with our application.
- To know which of your applications is most used by quality users. We can understand the current hits in the market from our portfolio, and start focusing on that application, giving it a higher priority than others.

The following screenshot demonstrates the use of the quality measure. This shows you how to create a funnel to get in-application purchases within three days:

Different businesses can have different parameters to measure user quality. Some of these parameters can be as follows:

1. Click on **Ad** and install the application. This filter helps to get the number of users those have installed the application and clicked on ads.

2. To get the statistics for the users who upgraded the application within one week of the trial

3. To get the count of users who have installed the application within one day of the trial

4. To get the location where the most users are installing the application

5. To know which user gender creates the major portion of your revenue

6. To know the language of users who majorly contribute to revenue

7. To know the type of the users who were cross-referenced between two or more of your applications

8. To know the upcoming trends for a particular user type

User acquisition

The strength of your user base is a prominent figure for any business. A user base basically comprises of customers or clients who fuel the business. If you get useful data to acquire quality users/clients/customers, what can be better than that? You can use data from Flurry to maintain user acquisition in following possible ways:

- To determine the channel/advertising source that is providing you with quality users
- To determine what your return of investment from a particular channel is
- To optimize future advertisement campaigns as per your requirements
- To target a portion of quality users determined in the next release
- To set up a location-specific campaign to get maximum user acquisition
- To extract the channel that can provide you maximum user coverage
- To determine and implement the latest trends in your application domain

User retention

What if you acquired a decent number of users and are not able to retain them? User retention is the most challenging concern these days. It has become more difficult because of increased competition, dynamic markets, and fast-paced technology changes.

There are various possibilities to use data provided by Flurry to nourish user retention in our business:

1. Determine and change the product as per the evolving trends. As we know, moving with the times and the world is crucial. We can use Flurry to keep ourselves updated in the market as Flurry provides data from a huge stack of Big Data and analysis of this data.

   Setting your focus on a positive customer group as per the data so that quality users are always there. There are a few groups of users whose retention gives us a lot of value; therefore, they can be focused on, instead of focusing on negative users.

The following screenshot demonstrates the output statistics generated from user retention data. These demographics help to better understand user behavior:

CATEGORY	AVERAGE USER RETENTION			FREQUENCY OF USE BY WEEK
	30 DAY	60 DAY	90 DAY	
Weather	73%	63%	55%	3.7
Reference	70%	61%	54%	3.4
Sports: Scores	67%	58%	51%	4.8
News	73%	57%	50%	5.2
Travel	60%	51%	45%	2.6
Lifestyle: Communication	62%	52%	44%	8.8
Utilities	62%	51%	43%	3.1
Games: Single Player	62%	49%	41%	3.8
Sports: Stat Trackers	60%	49%	41%	3.3
Books	56%	46%	39%	3.5
Food & Drink	55%	45%	39%	2.0
Navigation	57%	46%	38%	3.9
Finance: Banking	57%	45%	36%	3.7
Business	52%	42%	35%	2.3
Productivity	49%	41%	35%	4.6

2. Customize your advertisement campaign to provide offers to keep users' interest and retain it. Users look for change or for something that is exciting. We can identify the behavior of such user groups and provide them with what they want, of course, in the interest of our business.

3. Identify the weak points that are shown in the statistics and improve our strategies to avoid user inconvenience.

4. At certain locations, users may frequently access their mobile web application. Flurry provides the growth rate data from which you can estimate user growth and thus, you can plan for infrastructure and service improvements at that location.

5. Identify user crowd concentration and improve reachability. For example, you can allot special cells and a dedicated technical support number for user-crowded locations where it is obvious that technical support is greatly required.

6. Identify user locations and provide local benefits, which may help to retain them. For example, our application can provide users with discount coupons for their nearest retailers.

7. Understand user behavior and customize the application to significantly satisfy your users. For example, if the majority of users use X feature more than Y or Z, we can make our X feature more prominent and quickly accessible in the application.

8. Identify the age group and provide flexibility as per their age. For example, you may identify that your major users are comprised of the young population. Using this, you can identify and provide a flexibility of 30 days extra usage for students.

9. Understand the current benchmark to estimate user expectations. With a high-level insight of the Big Data analysis metrics provided by Flurry, you can set a benchmark and see how far you are related to the market standards and with respect to your competitors. It will give you a significant raise in standard and user satisfaction, making them stick with you, as shown in the following screenshot:

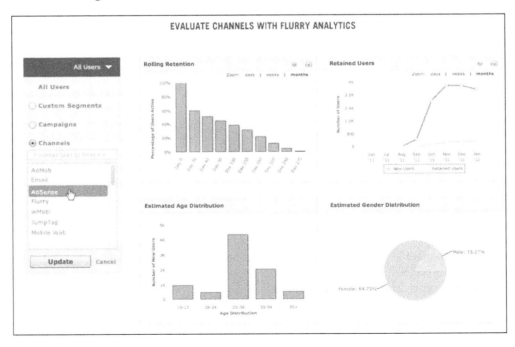

User engagement

Flurry Analytics gives you enough data and various custom and preset metrics for you to understand user behavior. User behavior and tracking their interaction with your application can help you to increasingly engage users with your application, giving them the complete worth of their time.

For example, your application may provide them with the latest stories, and the user may indulge more in a certain type of stories, such as suspense or real-life stories. You can start providing more options of these types to increase their engagement with your application. In this way, Flurry can help us to take decision for better user retention.

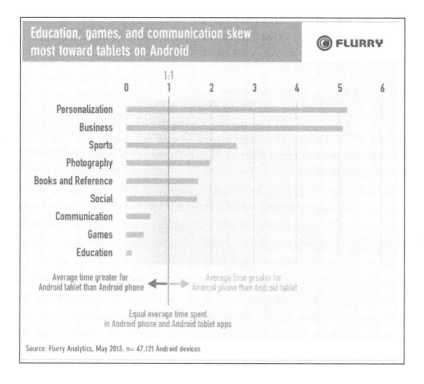

User monetization

We can use the data provided by Flurry to mine the information to gain actionable intelligence in the field of market research. We know where and how people use the application, and using this, we can monetize our users.

We can monetize our users in following ways:

- Increasing revenue from advertisements as a result of marketing information, mined from the data provided by Flurry.

- Applying charges after a certain limit of usage in various terms. For example, if your application exceeds more than 20 hits on your application program interface in an hour, you can charge a user.

- Providing the selected advertisement to get the maximum return on investment for clients who provide the advertisements.

- Cross-referencing one application with other concerns can increase the chance of monetizing users.

- Providing large user-based data as a paid upgrade can monetize your users significantly.

Platforms and devices

We can use data from Flurry to identify a positive platform for us. Flurry provides a measure for platform-specific users and their interaction with apps that are built over different platforms. There are various platforms such as Android, iOS, Bada, Windows, and Symbian. Similarly, there are different devices that the user can access Flurry from, as shown in the following screenshot:

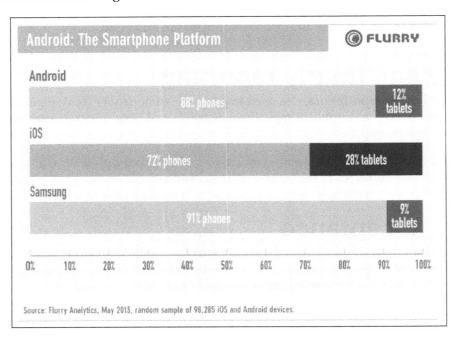

We can use the count of these users to determine the platform that should be focused on and targeted for advertisement and revenue generation.

Investors and sponsors

The data from Flurry can be used to prepare awesome presentations to attract investors and sponsors for your application. Flurry provides good demographic representation of data that can be very useful for the marketing team while pitching the application. Thus, with the usage of data, we can build trust by showing investors and sponsors how well the application is currently performing.

Crash detection

Let's think about a developer's perspective of using Flurry. It not only eases the life of the installer, but also that of the developers to identify the root cause of a crash. As discussed in *Chapter 3*, *Data Analytics*, Flurry data can be used to debug your code and find the point of failure quickly.

Alerts

You can use Flurry as an emergency alert tool that will promptly inform you if your your application has any mishap. This in turn will reduce your reaction time and avoid a loss of production hours and millions in sales/revenue.

Daily and hourly reporting

Daily and hourly reporting can be used to generate an hourly or daily report that maintains a history of application performance and real-time decision-making processes for the application.

Similarly, you will know the number of active users in your application at any point in time, which helps a lot in taking dynamic decisions.

User acceptance

The data from Flurry gives us deep insights into the application version that is highly accepted by the user. It can be very useful for you to know the most popular version. This data can be used in further releases as well.

Summary

In this chapter, we learned and how to use data provided by Flurry to improve our business and marketing.

We came across various areas where this data can be used to enhance the application's presence on the market.

We have learned about the various ways to use of analytics data for our benefit and strong management controls.

Index

Symbols

T

time filter 60
time spent
  tracking 26, 27
Top Carriers statistics 56
Total Errors graph 57
Total Events 25

U

UIImage class 59
Unique Device ID (UDID) 30
Unique Users Performing Event 24
Urban Airship 59
user
  accepting 68
  engaging, ways 66
  monetizing, ways 67

User Acquisition

User Acquisition
  analyzing 42-44
  data using, ways 63
User Acquisition tab 43
user quality
  measuring 61
  measuring, parameters 62
user retention
  nourishing 63-65
users details 30, 31
Users filter 59

V

VERSIONNAME parameter 54
versions
  tracking 28, 29
versions filter 60

Thank you for buying
Getting Started with Flurry Analytics

About Packt Publishing

Packt, pronounced 'packed', published its first book "Mastering phpMyAdmin for Effective MySQL Management" in April 2004 and subsequently continued to specialize in publishing highly focused books on specific technologies and solutions.

Our books and publications share the experiences of your fellow IT professionals in adapting and customizing today's systems, applications, and frameworks. Our solution based books give you the knowledge and power to customize the software and technologies you're using to get the job done. Packt books are more specific and less general than the IT books you have seen in the past. Our unique business model allows us to bring you more focused information, giving you more of what you need to know, and less of what you don't.

Packt is a modern, yet unique publishing company, which focuses on producing quality, cutting-edge books for communities of developers, administrators, and newbies alike. For more information, please visit our website: www.packtpub.com.

About Packt Enterprise

In 2010, Packt launched two new brands, Packt Enterprise and Packt Open Source, in order to continue its focus on specialization. This book is part of the Packt Enterprise brand, home to books published on enterprise software – software created by major vendors, including (but not limited to) IBM, Microsoft and Oracle, often for use in other corporations. Its titles will offer information relevant to a range of users of this software, including administrators, developers, architects, and end users.

Writing for Packt

We welcome all inquiries from people who are interested in authoring. Book proposals should be sent to author@packtpub.com. If your book idea is still at an early stage and you would like to discuss it first before writing a formal book proposal, contact us; one of our commissioning editors will get in touch with you.

We're not just looking for published authors; if you have strong technical skills but no writing experience, our experienced editors can help you develop a writing career, or simply get some additional reward for your expertise.

Scaling Big Data with Hadoop and Solr

ISBN: 978-1-78328-137-4   Paperback: 144 pages

Learn exciting new ways to build efficient, high performance enterprise search repositories for Big Data using Hadoop and Solr

1. Understand the different approaches of making Solr work on Big Data as well as the benefits and drawbacks

2. Learn from interesting, real-life use cases for Big Data search along with sample code

3. Work with the Distributed Enterprise Search without prior knowledge of Hadoop and Solr

Fast Data Processing with Spark

ISBN: 978-1-78216-706-8   Paperback: 120 pages

High-speed distributed computing made easy with Spark

1. Implement Spark's interactive shell to prototype distributed applications

2. Deploy Spark jobs to various clusters such as Mesos, EC2, Chef, YARN, EMR, and so on

3. Use Shark's SQL query-like syntax with Spark

Please check **www.PacktPub.com** for information on our titles

Getting Started with Greenplum for Big Data Analytics

Getting Started with Greenplum
for Big Data Analytics

A hands-on guide on how to execute an analytics project from
conceptualization to operationalization using Greenplum

Foreword by V. Laxmikanth, Managing Director, Broadridge Financial
Solutions (India) Private Limited

Sunila Gollapudi   [PACKT] enterprise

Getting Started with Greenplum for Big Data Analytics

ISBN: 978-1-78217-704-3   Paperback: 172 pages

A hands-on-guide on how to execute an analytics
project from conceptualization to operationalization
using Greenplum

1. Explore the software components and appliance
   modules available in Greenplum

2. Learn core Big Data Architecture concepts and
   master data loading and processing patterns

3. Understand Big Data problems and the Data
   Science lifecycle

**Big Data Analytics with
R and Hadoop**

Set up an integrated infrastructure of R and Hadoop to turn your
data analytics into Big Data analytics

Vignesh Prajapati   [PACKT] open source

Big Data Analytics with R and Hadoop

ISBN: 978-1-78216-328-2   Paperback: 238 pages

Set up an integrated infrastructure of R and Hadoop
to turn your data analytics into Big Data analytics

1. Write Hadoop MapReduce within R

2. Learn data analytics with R and the
   Hadoop platform

3. Handle HDFS data within R

4. Understand Hadoop streaming with R

5. Encode and enrich datasets into R

Please check **www.PacktPub.com** for information on our titles